Haydn Richards
Junior English

BOOK 2

Illustrated by George A. Craig

GINN AND COMPANY LTD
18 BEDFORD ROW   LONDON WC1

© Haydn Richards, 1965
Fifth impression 1970
157010
SBN 602 20498 4

MADE AND PRINTED IN GREAT BRITAIN BY
C. TINLING & CO. LTD., LONDON AND PRESCOT

PREFACE

The main aim of HAYDN RICHARDS JUNIOR ENGLISH is to enable the pupil to work alone, as far as is possible. For this reason complete lists of the words needed to answer the various exercises are given. Being thus provided with the necessary tools the pupil should experience little difficulty in doing the work.

The course provides ample and varied practice in all the English topics usually taught in the Junior School. Such simple grammatical terms as are essential to the understanding of the language are introduced at appropriate stages, together with simple definitions, lucid explanations and easy examples.

The meaning of every proverb and idiom dealt with is given, so that these may be used correctly in both writing and conversation.

A noteworthy feature of each book in the series is the detailed alphabetical Contents facilitating reference to any particular topic by the teacher and the older pupils.

In addition to teaching and testing such topics as Parts of Speech, Opposites, Synonyms, Homonyms, Punctuation, Direct and Indirect Speech, Sentence Linkage and Structure, etc., the course includes verbal intelligence exercises designed to stimulate clear thinking, so that by the end of the fourth year the pupil who has worked steadily through the course is well equipped for any entrance examination.

H. R.

CONTENTS

Nouns (Naming Words)

Read: The dog followed the boy.
dog is the **name** of an animal.
boy is the **name** of a person.

A noun is the name of a person or thing.

A Look for the nouns in these sentences. Write them in your book.

1. The window was broken.
2. I lost my knife.
3. This pencil is too short.
4. The cake was stale.
5. The bird flew away.
6. We bought a bat and ball.
7. The dog barked at the tramp.
8. Summer is the warmest season.
9. Boys and girls come out to play.
10. Only one apple was left on the dish.

B Name three things you might find in—

1. a toy shop
2. a farmyard
3. a kitchen
4. a railway station
5. a motor-car
6. a hospital
7. a cinema
8. a church

Use your dictionary

Verbs (Doing Words)

The butcher cut the meat and weighed it.

The words **cut** and **weighed** tell what the butcher **did** to the meat.

These are **doing** words, or **action** words.

A verb is a word which shows action.

A Find the verbs in these sentences. Write them in your book.

1. The little girl cried.
2. We cut a lot of wood for the fire.
3. Please pass me the jam.
4. Roy knocked at the door of the office.
5. Two robins hopped on to the sill of the window.
6. Pam put her toys away and went to bed.
7. After school John cycles to the park and plays cricket.
8. The clown smiled when we waved to him.
9. Henry told his mother that he liked her cakes.
10. Carol ate four sweets and gave the rest away.

B Name three actions which might be done by each of these persons.

Example: 1. a baby   cry, play, suck

1. a baby
2. a footballer
3. your teacher
4. a gardener
5. a cricketer
6. your mother
7. a pupil in your class
8. a farmer

Vowels

Always write **an** before words beginning with

a   e   i   o   u

These letters are called **vowels**.

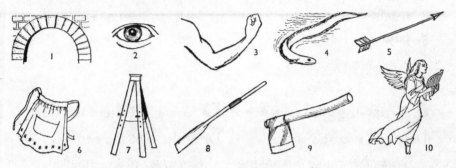

A Write the names of these things, putting **an** before each. You will find them in this list.

angel	apron	arch	arm	arrow
axe	easel	eel	eye	oar

B Write **a** or **an** before each of these words.

1. — book
2. — ant
3. — inch
4. — rock
5. — oval
6. — end
7. — flag
8. — inn
9. — chair
10. — organ
11. — ox
12. — elf
13. — sweet
14. — hat
15. — imp
16. — shoe

C Write **a** or **an** to finish the sentences.

1. Pauline ate — apple and — banana.
2. Mother gave — order for a new dress.
3. We came to — lake with — island in the middle.
4. Linda is spending — holiday with — aunt in London.
5. — east wind is colder than — west wind.

Verbs (Adding -ED and -ING)

A Write **-ing** after each word.   **B** Write **-ed** after each word.

1. look	6. go	1. stay	6. touch
2. walk	7. read	2. post	7. help
3. push	8. camp	3. work	8. fill
4. teach	9. wear	4. lock	9. end
5. pay	10. roast	5. rush	10. turn

C Write **-ing** after each word.   **D** Write **-ed** after each word.
Drop the **e** at the end.   Drop the **e** at the end.

Example: smoke – smoking   *Example:* place – placed

1. smoke	6. waste	1. place	6. blame
2. dance	7. raise	2. live	7. snore
3. dare	8. hope	3. rattle	8. close
4. love	9. blaze	4. hate	9. taste
5. share	10. serve	5. chase	10. stroke

E Write the missing words by adding **-ing** or **-ed** to the verbs in heavy type.

1. We saw a small dog — a cat. (**chase**)
2. The fire — when a log was put on it. (**blaze**)
3. He has been — in Torquay for nearly a year. (**live**)
4. The old man was — most of the night. (**snore**)
5. Nobody — to answer the door. (**dare**)
6. Paul sat on the rug — the cat. (**stroke**)
7. Everybody — the Queen would visit the town. (**hope**)
8. We got there just as the shop was — (**close**)

Adjectives (Describing Words)

Read: The queen of the fairies had a golden wand.
The word **golden** tells us **what kind** of **wand**
it was.

Because it describes the noun **wand**, we call it an
adjective.

> **An adjective is a word which describes a noun.**

A Pick out and write the adjectives in these sentences.

1. A big lorry was parked outside the school.
2. The rough sea upset the boys.
3. Claire wore a lovely frock at the party.
4. The baby was playing with a plastic doll.
5. The torch gave a brilliant light.
6. The captain of the ship had a wooden leg.
7. It was easy to wade through the shallow river.
8. We helped the blind man across the road.
9. It was such a busy street.
10. At the circus we saw a clever monkey riding a bicycle.

B Put these adjectives in their proper places below.

loud	heavy	deep	white	leather
tidy	juicy	sharp	savage	beautiful

1. a — doll
2. a — knife
3. a — noise
4. a — dog
5. a — shower
6. a — pear
7. a — belt
8. a — room
9. a — sheet
10. a — cut

Cinderella

Cinderella ran to the garden and brought her godmother the finest pumpkin she could find, wondering how this would help her to go to the ball.

The godmother scooped out the inside of the pumpkin, leaving nothing but the rind. Then she touched it with her magic wand, and the pumpkin was changed in a moment into a fine coach, all shining with gold.

After that she went to look into the mouse-trap, where she found six mice, all alive. She told Cinderella to lift the trap-door up a little, and as each mouse came out she gave it a tap with her wand. At once it was changed into a beautiful horse. This made a very fine team of six horses, all dappled grey in colour.

(*Tales from Perrault*)

1. What did the godmother do with the pumpkin?
2. With what did she touch the pumpkin?
3. What happened when she did this?
4. What did the godmother find in the mouse-trap?
5. What did she tell Cinderella to do?
6. What did the godmother do as each mouse came out?
7. What happened to each mouse?
8. What was the colour of each horse?

Questions

Every question must have a question mark (?) at the end.

Examples: Why were you so late?
Where have you been?

Use the words in the list to fill the spaces in the questions below.

Remember to put a question mark (?) at the end of each question.

A

| why | who | how | what | whose |
| have | when | did | which | where |

1. — you enjoy the tea
2. — are you today
3. — told you about the party
4. — were you absent yesterday
5. — did you have for dinner
6. — are you coming to see me
7. — of these books do you like best
8. — has mother put the sweets
9. — cap is this
10. — you been to London

B Write five sentences of your own, each beginning with one of the words from the list above.

8

The Weather

When the weather is wet,
We must not fret.
When the weather is cold,
We must not scold.

When the weather is warm
We must not storm,
But be thankful together
Whatever the weather.

A The words in the list are used to describe weather. Write these sentences in your book, filling each space with a word from the list.

breezy	foggy	rainy	misty	showery
stormy	sunny	windy	icy	thundery

1. When the wind is blowing hard it is —.
2. When the sun is shining it is —.
3. When there is a fog it is —.
4. When there is a mist it is —.
5. When the rain pours it is a — day.
6. When there is a storm it is —.
7. When there is a breeze it is —.
8. When there is thunder it is —.
9. When there are showers the weather is —.
10. When the wind is as cold as ice it is —.

B Write two or three sentences about any two of these.

1. a sunny morning
2. a cold afternoon
3. a wet afternoon
4. a windy day
5. a stormy sea
6. a foggy night

Using the Right Word

is	The wind **is** cold.	is	This apple **is** sour. (*one*)
his	Tom lost **his** book.	are	These apples **are** sour. (*more than one*)
as	You are **as** tall **as** Janet.	was	The boy **was** happy. (*one*)
has	Anne **has** a new coat.	were	The boys **were** happy. (*more than one*)
did	He **did** his work well.	saw	We **saw** the Tower of London.
done	He has **done** his work well. (*helping word:* **has**)	seen	We have **seen** the Tower of London. (*helping word:* **have**)

A Choose the right word to fill each space.
1. He can't run because — leg — stiff. (**is; his**)
2. The boy — afraid of the bull. (**was; were**)
3. Several cows — grazing in the field. (**was; were**)
4. She cannot come — she — too much work to do. (**as; has**)
5. Roger — going to visit — grandmother. (**is; his**)
6. Joy — a lump — big — an egg on her forehead. (**as; has**)

B Write the word which will fill each gap.
1. Three people — the accident. (**saw; seen**)
2. Sarah — her best to tidy the room. (**did; done**)
3. The book — kept on the shelf. (**is; are**)
4. Philip rested when he had — his work. (**did; done**)
5. It is the biggest trout I have —. (**saw; seen**)
6. The books — kept on the shelf. (**is; are**)

10

Words With More Than One Meaning

Some words have more than one meaning.

Examples: The brown **bear** climbed the tree.
Sandra could hardly **bear** the pain.

Use the word in the list to fill the spaces in the sentences.
The same word must be used for each pair of sentences.

bark	blow	chest	fair	kind
light	match	ring	shed	watch

1. The lawn mower is kept in the garden —.
   Many trees — their leaves in the autumn.

2. The — woman gave the beggar ten pence (10p).
   This is a different — of toffee.

3. It is time to — the school bell.
   The wedding — was made of solid gold.

4. The oak tree has a rough —.
   The dog began to — when the children teased him.

5. Much damage is done when high winds —.
   A — on the head knocked the boxer out.

6. Shirley has very — hair.
   There were many amusements at the —.

7. My new — keeps very good time.
   We did not — television last night.

8. The parcel was as — as a feather.
   In winter we — the fire every day.

9. There was a big crowd at the football —.
   Father struck a — and lit his pipe.

10. James has a cold on his —.
    The tools are kept in a big wooden —.

Using Capital Letters

Capital letters are used:

1. to begin a sentence.
   Always start a sentence with a capital letter.

2. to begin every line of poetry.
   The world is so full of a number of things
   I'm sure we should all be as happy as kings.

3. for the names of people and pets.
   George, Jennifer, Fluffy, Pongo
   Also for **Mr., Mrs., Dr.**

4. for the names of places, rivers, mountains and so on.
   Bristol, Thames, Snowdon, Atlantic

5. for addresses.
   29 South Road, Bradford.

6. for the names of the days of the week.
   Monday, Wednesday, Saturday

7. for the word I.
   I did my best but I failed.

Copy these sentences, using capital letters where they are needed.

1. henry chaplin lives in hastings.

2. the world's best cutlery is made in sheffield.

3. david and i are going to london for a day.

4. we hope to go next friday.

5. the highest mountain in wales is snowdon.

6. canterbury is in kent.

7. a new shop has opened in bond street.

8. up into the cherry tree
   who should go but little me?

9. colin has a pet dog named rover.

10. we paid a visit to mr. and mrs. reeve.

The Storks

On the last house in a village was a storks' nest. The stork-mother sat in the nest with her four little ones. A little way off, on the ridge of the roof, stood the stork-father, with one leg drawn up under him. It seemed almost as if he were carved in wood, so still did he stand.

In the street below a troop of children were playing; and when they saw the storks, first one of the boldest of them, and afterwards all together, sang the old rhyme about the storks.

> "Storks, storks, fly home I beg,
> And don't stay idling on one leg.
> There's your wife sits in her nest,
> Rocking all her young to rest.
>
> The first will be hung,
> The second roasted young,
> They'll come and shoot the third,
> And stab the fourth, I've heard."

1. Where was the storks' nest?
2. How many young ones were in the nest?
3. Where did the stork-father stand?
4. How was he standing?
5. What did the children in the street below do when they saw the storks?
6. What did the children say would happen to the third little stork?
7. Which of the storks would be roasted young?
8. What would happen to the first little stork?

HERE and HEAR

here	means **in this place**
	I left the bag **here** five minutes ago.
hear	We could **hear** the thrushes singing.
	You **hear** with your **ear**.

A Write **here** or **hear** in each space.

1. Will you stay — till I come back?
2. Ann did not — her mother calling her.
3. We could — someone snoring in the next room.
4. — is the ball you were looking for.
5. Would you like to live —?
6. Deaf people cannot —.

THERE and THEIR

there	means **in that place**.
	He lives over **there**.
their	means **belonging to them**.
	The boys played with **their** football.

B Write **there** or **their** in each space.

1. Children should obey — parents.
2. I waited — for nearly an hour.
3. — are a hundred pence in a pound.
4. Wise parents buy books as presents for — children.
5. The two boys went to the show with — father.
6. I saw patches of clover here and — on the lawn.

Plurals

Singular means **ONE.**   boy; glass; daisy; leaf

Plural means **MORE THAN ONE.**   boys; glasses; daisies; leaves

A Add **-s** to each word to form the plural.

1. bird
2. cook
3. head
4. farmer
5. tree
6. chair
7. river
8. coat

B Add **-es** to each word to form the plural.

1. bush
2. inch
3. coach
4. brush
5. box
6. dish
7. church
8. match

C Change **y** to **i** and add **-es.**

1. fly
2. pony
3. baby
4. berry
5. story
6. lady
7. gipsy
8. penny

D Change **f** to **v** and add **-es.**

1. elf
2. shelf
3. loaf
4. half
5. calf
6. leaf
7. wolf
8. sheaf

E Copy these sentences, making each noun in heavy type plural.

Example: 1. They fed the calves on milk.

1. They fed the **calf** on milk.
2. The **butcher** sharpened the **knife**.
3. The **baker** put the burnt **loaf** on the **shelf**.
4. The **gardener** trimmed the **bush**.
5. The **gipsy** fed the **pony**.
6. The **leaf** fell from the **tree**.
7. The **fly** buzzed round the **baby**.
8. The **sweep** put the **brush** in the **box**.

Verbs (Adding -ED and -ING)

When we add **-ed** or **-ing** to each of the words in this list we double the last letter.

nod	hum	drop	grin
nodded	hummed	dropped	grinned
nodding	humming	dropping	grinning

A Add **-ing** to each word, first doubling the last letter.

1. peg
2. chat
3. rob
4. stab
5. hum
6. skim
7. drop
8. skid
9. drag
10. slip

B Add **-ed** to each word, first doubling the last letter.

1. snap
2. grin
3. lap
4. rub
5. nod
6. dip
7. trim
8. grab
9. slam
10. drip

C Fill each space with the right verb.

1. Water was — from a hole in the can.
2. The car — on the wet road and crashed.
3. Joy — a merry tune as she went along.
4. Mother — the wet clothes on the line.
5. The rude boy — the door as he went out.
6. Alan — on a banana skin and hurt his leg.
7. The gardener was busy — the hedge.
8. A lovely white kitten was — a saucer of milk.

16

Joining Sentences (so)

You have learnt how to join sentences using the words **and** or **but** as links.

Father poked the fire. He put coal on it. (*two sentences*)

Father poked the fire **and** put coal on it. (*one sentence*)

We looked for the book. We failed to find it. (*two sentences*)

We looked for the book **but** failed to find it. (*one sentence*)

The word **so** is also used as a link.

It started to rain. We went home. (*two sentences*)

It started to rain **so** we went home. (*one sentence*)

Join each pair of sentences by using the word **so**.

1. It was a fine day. We went down to the beach.
2. Paul had lost his bus fare. He had to walk home.
3. The old man was tired. He sat down to rest.
4. The children had mumps. They could not go to school.
5. Bill had no money. He could not buy a lollipop.
6. Charles felt hot. He took his coat off.
7. The weather was wet. We wore our Wellingtons.
8. The blind man was afraid to cross the road. We helped him.
9. The tie was too dear. We did not buy it.
10. The soil in the garden was very wet. The gardener could not dig it.

Forming Nouns

Some nouns are formed by adding **-ness** to words.

sad	slow	deaf	stout
sadness	slowness	deafness	stoutness

When **-ness** is added to words ending with **y**, the **y** is changed to **i**.

steady	shabby	sleepy
steadiness	shabbiness	sleepiness

A Add **-ness** to these words.

1. glad
2. stale
3. quick
4. tired
5. loud
6. greedy
7. lame
8. blind
9. rough
10. fresh
11. sore
12. sad
13. giddy
14. wicked
15. good

B Fill each space with the noun formed from the word in brackets.

1. Jennie thanked her teacher for her —. (**kind**)
2. There was thick — over the land. (**dark**)
3. Winter often brings much —. (**ill**)
4. It is — to speed on busy roads. (**mad**)
5. The wood was two centimetres in —. (**thick**)
6. The old man was suffering from —. (**weak**)
7. We were surprised at the — of the performing lions. (**tame**)
8. The man's — was caused by an explosion. (**deaf**)
9. Mrs. Platt scolded Bobby for his —. (**lazy**)
10. Gerald has a — for strawberries. (**fond**)

The Sleeping Beauty

The Prince entered a room all covered with gold, where he saw upon a bed a beautiful princess about fifteen or sixteen years old, whose beauty was quite charming.

He approached her, trembling, and silent with wonder, and knelt down before her. Then, as the spell of the fairy was at an end, the Princess woke, and, looking at him tenderly, she said:

"Is it you, my Prince? You have been a long time coming."

The Prince, charmed with these words, and much more by the manner in which they were spoken, did not know how to show his love and thanks. He told her that he loved her better than himself. They talked for four hours, and yet they had not said half the things they wanted to say.

1. The room was all — with —.
2. The Princess was — or — years old.
3. Her beauty was quite —.
4. The Prince — down — her.
5. When the — of the fairy ended the Princess —.
6. She looked at the Prince —.
7. She — him that he had been a long — coming.
8. The — told the — that he loved her — than —.
9. They talked for — hours.
10. They could not say — the things they — to say.

Adjectives (Describing Words)

Adjectives can be formed by adding **-y** to some words.

rust	greed	wealth	storm
rusty	greedy	wealthy	stormy

A What are the missing words?

1. Hands covered with dirt — hands
2. A day of strong winds a — day
3. A mountain with many rocks a — mountain
4. A beach covered with sand a — beach
5. A table covered with dust a — table
6. A chest covered with hair a — chest
7. Hair which has curls — hair
8. Food which has a lot of salt — food
9. A sky with many clouds a — sky
10. A girl who has lots of luck a — girl

When **-y** is added to some words the last letter of the word is doubled.

sun	fog	skin	fur	bag
sunny	foggy	skinny	furry	baggy

When **-y** is added to a word ending with **e** this letter is dropped.

noise	smoke	ease	shade	stone
noisy	smoky	easy	shady	stony

B What are the missing adjectives?

1. a — day (**sun**)
2. an — chair (**ease**)
3. a — hand (**skin**)
4. a — animal (**fur**)
5. a — chimney (**smoke**)
6. a — class (**noise**)
7. — trousers (**bag**)
8. a — tree (**shade**)
9. a — path (**stone**)
10. a — night (**fog**)

Verbs (Adding -ES and -ED)

> I **try** hard.   He **tries** hard.   She **tried** hard.

When **-es** or **-ed** is added to a verb ending with **y**, this letter is first changed to **i**.

A Copy and fill in the missing letters.

1. try   . . . es
2. cry   . . . ed
3. dry   . . . ed
4. fry   . . . es
5. spy   . . . ed
6. dirty   . . . . . es
7. copy   . . . . ed
8. empty   . . . . . es
9. hurry   . . . . . ed
10. carry   . . . . . es

B Finish each sentence by using the right form of the verb in brackets, adding **-es** or **-ed** as needed.

1. Mother . . . . . bacon and eggs for my breakfast this morning. (**fry**)
2. Every day Ann . . . . . . sums from Angela. (**copy**)
3. She . . . . . because she had cut her knee. (**cry**)
4. Although we . . . . to the station we missed the train. (**hurry**)
5. Again and again the little spider . . . . . to climb up the thread. (**try**)
6. David . . . . . . his books to school in a satchel. (**carry**)
7. Every time she washes her hands she . . . . . them well. (**dry**)
8. Yesterday the dustmen . . . . all the bins in our street. (**empty**)
9. I . . . . . a rook up on the church tower. (**spy**)
10. Mark . . . . . . his hands so he went to wash them. (**dirty**)

Same Sound—Different Meaning

Some words have the same sound as other words, but they are different in spelling and meaning.

Look at these four pairs of words.

bare	A **bare** tree has no leaves.
bear	The polar **bear** is a very big animal.
dear	The dress was too **dear** so she did not buy it. Alan's mother is very **dear** to him.
deer	A **deer** is a graceful animal.
fair	**Fair** hair is light in colour. We had fun at the **fair**.
fare	The bus conductor asked me for my **fare**.
heel	The back part of your foot is called the **heel**.
heal	To **heal** a person means to make him well.

Write the word which fills the gap.

1. The bus — to school is three pence (3p). (**fair; fare**)

2. The cut on your finger will soon —. (**heel; heal**)

3. Wendy's pet was a — little white rabbit. (**deer; dear**)

4. The big brown — sat up and begged. (**bear; bare**)

5. The — of the woman's shoe came right off. (**heel; heal**)

6. Peter won a coconut at the —. (**fair; fare**)

7. Many trees are — in winter. (**bear; bare**)

8. We saw ten — in the park. (**dear; deer**)

22

Full Stops

A **full stop** is put at the end of every telling sentence.
>*Example:* I hung my coat on the coat-hanger.

A **question mark** is put at the end of every question.
>*Example:* Did you hang your coat on the coat-hanger?

A Copy each sentence. Put a full stop or a question mark at the end of each.

1. The bushy tail of a fox is called a brush
2. A camel can go for days without water
3. Have you visited the Tower of London
4. The Nile is a long river in Africa
5. Will you call for me in the morning
6. Our school starts at nine o'clock
7. Did you post the letter I gave you
8. Beavers can gnaw through big trees

Commas

When the names of three or more things come together, we separate them by using **commas.** (,)

Example: For tea we had cakes, jelly, fruit and trifle.

Notice that there is no comma between the last two things. The word **and** separates them.

B Copy these sentences. Put in the commas.

1. Robert Andrew Michael and Peter were ill.
2. The fishmonger had hake plaice herrings mackerel and cod.
3. London York Birmingham and Exeter are all cities.
4. The colours of the rainbow are red orange yellow green blue indigo and violet.
5. At the zoo we saw lions tigers elephants camels and monkeys.

Similars

A **wealthy** man   A **rich** man

The words **wealthy** and **rich** have much the same meaning.
Learn the list of similars before answering the questions.

collect . . gather	commence. . begin	drowsy . .sleepy
difficult .hard	hasten . . . . .hurry	naked . . .bare
pile. . . . .heap	peril. . . . . . .danger	plucky. . .brave
	weeping. . . .crying	

A Write a simpler word in place of each word in heavy type.

1. The concert will **commence** at 7 o'clock.
2. Jill found the sum very **difficult**.
3. The ship was in great **peril**.
4. A **pile** of stones lay outside the school.
5. The **plucky** sailor saved the boy's life.
6. At the funeral several women were **weeping**.
7. Sitting near a big fire makes one **drowsy**.
8. The sun shone on the bather's **naked** back.

B In each line find the word which is **similar** in meaning
to the word in capital letters.

1. DROWSY   lively   quick   active   sleepy
2. HASTEN   fix   hurry   work   play
3. COLLECT   give   spend   gather   climb
4. DIFFICULT   clever   easy   hard   simple
5. PERIL   danger   length   safety   depth
6. PLUCKY   silly   brave   short   noisy
7. ASSIST   help   coax   hinder   wait
8. HALT   hurry   linger   run   stop

Tom and the Otters

As Tom was sitting on a water-lily leaf watching the gnats dance, he heard the strangest noise up the stream. He looked up the water, and there he saw a great ball rolling over and over down the stream, seeming one moment of soft brown fur, and the next of shining glass.

And when he came near, the ball turned out to be four or five beautiful creatures, many times larger than Tom, who were swimming about, and rolling and diving and twisting in the most charming fashion. Tom did not know that they were otters at play.

But when the biggest of them saw Tom, she darted out from the rest, and cried in the water-language sharply enough, "Quick, children, here is something to eat!" and came at poor Tom showing a wicked pair of eyes and a set of sharp teeth. But Tom slipped in between the water-lily roots as fast as he could, and then turned round and made faces at her.

(*The Water Babies*—Charles Kingsley)

1. Where was Tom sitting when this happened?
2. What was he watching?
3. What did he hear up the stream?
4. What did Tom see rolling over and over down the stream?
5. Name two things that it looked like.
6. What did the beautiful creatures turn out to be?
7. Name four things which these creatures were doing.
8. How did Tom escape from them?

Fun With Words

In each line below there are two pairs of words and one odd word.

You have to find the word which will make up the third pair.

Look at the first pair of words in line 1. **ear, hear**

The second word is made by writing the letter **h** before the first word.

Look at the second pair. The second word is again formed by writing **h** before the first word. **at, hat**

To find the missing word write **h** before the odd word.
arm, harm

A Now find the other missing words. In every line a different letter must be added.

1. ear, hear	at, hat	arm, —
2. all, ball	eat, beat	oil, —
3. ark, park	ink, pink	lay, —
4. ill, mill	ask, mask	other, —
5. old, gold	lad, glad	race, —

B In each line below the same letter ends the first word and begins the second. Write the ten pairs of words.

Example: 1. SAT TEA

1. SA .	. EA		6. POS .	. RAP
2. BE .	. OG		7. FIL .	. IFT
3. SH .	. GG		8. GOO .	. OOR
4. BI .	. UN		9. HEA .	. ICH
5. WA .	. LY		10. HEL .	. LAY

Showing Ownership

I like Simon's new puppy.

The **'s** in Simon's shows that the puppy **belongs** to Simon. It is **his**. He **owns** it.

A Copy these in your book, putting in the **'** before the **s**.

1. the robin's breast
2. the sailor's cap
3. the horse's mane
4. the rabbit's tail
5. the old man's beard
6. the grocer's apron
7. the gipsy's caravan
8. the baby's rattle
9. the Queen's crown
10. the dog s collar

Look: the kite which belongs to Paul (*long way*)
Paul's kite (*short way*)

B Write these the short way.

1. the book belonging to Mary
2. the bat which belongs to Peter
3. the ribbon belonging to Ann
4. the watch which belongs to Father
5. the ring which belongs to Mother

Look: the wool of the sheep (*long way*)
the sheep's wool (*short way*)

C Write these the short way.

1. the fur of the cat
2. the den of the lion
3. the beak of the blackbird
4. the ears of the donkey
5. the horns of the cow

Pictures and Sentences

Look at picture number 1. Find the sentence which matches it. Write it in your book. Do the same with the other pictures and sentences.

The dog is chasing the cat.
The suitcase had several labels on it.
Inside the box was a lovely ring.
A vase of flowers stood on the table.
The boy is much taller than the girl.
There were two cows grazing in the meadow.
A little mouse was busy nibbling the cheese.
The man is taking his dog for a walk.
The woman was dusting the chair.

Alphabetical Order

Look at the alphabet.

a	b	c	d	e	f	g	h	i	j	k	l	m
n	o	p	q	r	s	t	u	v	w	x	y	z

A

1. Write the third letter of the alphabet.
2. Which letter is last but one?
3. Which letter comes between **j** and **l**?
4. Write the three letters of which **o** is the middle letter.
5. What are the missing letters?

> g h . j k . m n o . q .

B
Write each line of words in **a-b-c** or alphabetical order. Look at the first letter of each word.

1. head   train   before   food   also
2. look   ready   winter   another   small
3. green   water   cross   inch   pull
4. paint   teach   little   heart   alone
5. please   answer   mountain   young   under

C
In each of these lines all the words are in alphabetical order except one. Write the odd word in each line.

Example: Line 1. bicycle

1. night   orange   pretty   queen   bicycle
2. army   bread   colour   letter   doctor
3. early   dress   figure   garden   house
4. kitchen   length   window   mouse   north
5. beauty   heavy   ground   middle   season

Short Forms

You have learnt how to join two words one of which is **not**.

is not	was not	does not	has not
isn't	wasn't	doesn't	hasn't

Notice that the ' stands for the **o** which is left out.

We can also join **is** to another word in this way.

he is	she is	it is	who is
he's	she's	it's	who's
that is	what is	where is	there is
that's	what's	where's	there's

Remember that the ' stands for the **i** which is left out.

Write these sentences, joining the two words in heavy type in each.

1. Brian says **he is** too busy to play.
2. I think **that is** a lovely dress.
3. Carol is tall, and **she is** pretty, also.
4. Thank goodness **it is** a fine day.
5. We can't work when **there is** a noise in the room.
6. I can guess **what is** in the box.
7. I wonder **who is** going to the party tonight.
8. **It is** not raining now.
9. Roger **does not** like going to town.
10. The pears **are not** quite ripe.

Rhymes

Read this poem, then answer the questions.

A Spring Song

See the yellow catkins cover
All the slender willows over;
And on mossy banks so green
Star-like primroses are seen;
And their clustering leaves below,
White and purple violets grow.

Hark! the little lambs are bleating,
And the cawing rooks are meeting
In the elms—a noisy crowd;
And all the birds are singing loud,
There, the first white butterfly
In the sun goes flitting by.

Mary Howitt

1. Write the word which rhymes with **meeting**.

2. Which word rhymes with **seen**?

3. **Grow** rhymes with **below**. Write three other words which rhyme with these two.

4. Give the word which rhymes with **over**.

5. Which two words in the poem rhyme with **proud**?

6. Write the word which rhymes with the name of an insect in the poem.

7. Which two words end with the same sound as **greeting**?

8. Write three words beginning with **c**, **d** and **f** which rhyme with **by**.

Noises of Animals

I bark   I roar   I crow   I bleat   I low

I bray   I mew   I grunt   I cluck   I growl

A Write the missing words.

1. sheep —
2. pigs —
3. dogs —
4. bears —
5. donkeys —

6. cockerels —
7. hens —
8. cats —
9. cows —
10. lions —

B Fill each space with the name of the creature or the name of the noise it makes.

1. The dog was — at a gipsy.
2. We heard the cows — in the meadow.
3. The — growled as the hunter raised his gun.
4. The loud braying of a — frightened the children.
5. The cat was — because she had hurt her paw.
6. The — bleated as the dog rounded them up.
7. The boys were up before the — started crowing.
8. The — roared when the keeper came to feed him.
9. Robert's brown — clucked after laying an egg.
10. The — grunted as he ate his food.

Verbs

I **like** apples.　　Sally **likes** apples.　　We both **like** apples.

I, you, we, they	he, she, it	I, you, we, they	he, she, it
do	does	play	plays
go	goes	say	says
put	puts	try	tries
run	runs	carry	carries
pull	pulls	hurry	hurries

A Copy and fill in the missing verb.

1. they — (**go; goes**)
2. I — (**try; tries**)
3. he — (**pull; pulls**)
4. you — (**say; says**)
5. we — (**do; does**)
6. she — (**put; puts**)
7. you — (**hurry; hurries**)
8. it — (**run; runs**)
9. I — (**carry; carries**)
10. they — (**play; plays**)

B Write the verb in the list above which will fill each space.

1. The children — football every day.
2. Mr. Gold — his umbrella on his arm.
3. Judith — her knitting by the fire.
4. We — to school five days a week.
5. Peter — his prayers every night.
6. I will catch the bus if I —.
7. Our cat always — after a mouse.
8. Sheila — hard to write a good letter.

C Write sentences of your own showing how each of these words can be used.

1. make; makes
2. eat; eats
3. read; reads
4. think; thinks
5. walk; walks
6. learn; learns

Writing Letters

> 9 High Street,
> Hanford.
> 12th July, 1964
>
> Dear Bernard,
>
> Next Friday is my birthday.
> Mother is giving me a lovely party. We shall
> all be glad if you will come.
>
> Tea will be at four o'clock, and
> there will be games and fireworks afterwards.
> The party will end at about seven o'clock.
>
> Your friend,
> Tom Weller

A Read the letter which Tom Weller wrote to his friend Bernard Baxter inviting him to his birthday party. Tom's mother showed him how to arrange the letter and how to address the envelope.

Pretend you are Bernard Baxter and that you have just had this letter from Tom Weller.

Write a letter to him thanking him for his kind invitation and telling him that you will be delighted to come.

> Master Bernard Baxter,
> 25 Victoria Terrace,
> HANFORD.

Draw an envelope and address it to Tom. You will find his address at the top of his letter.

B Pretend that you have been to Tom's party. Write a letter to another friend who was not there telling him how much you enjoyed yourself. Say what you had to eat, what games you played and what fireworks you saw.

Draw an envelope and address it to your friend.

Opposites (Using UN)

well **unwell** **broken** **unbroken**

Some words are given an opposite meaning by writing **un** before them.

Look at the words below the pictures.

A Form the opposites of these words by using **un**.

1. happy	4. seen	7. tie	10. real
2. willing	5. do	8. wise	11. safe
3. paid	6. screw	9. roll	12. steady

B Choose any six of the words you have made and use them in sentences of your own.

C Copy these sentences, adding **un** to the words in heavy type to give them an opposite meaning.

1. The new road is **finished**.
2. The doctor said that Martin was a **healthy** boy.
3. The pears were **ripe**.
4. The dealer was **fair** in his dealings.
5. Jennie was **kind** to her friends.
6. Father could not **lock** the drawer.
7. The room had an **even** floor.
8. The man was **known** to the police.

Collections

A number of **sheep** together is called a **flock**.

A number of **tools** together is called a **set**.

a bunch of grapes	a herd of cattle
a chest of drawers	a pack of wolves
a crowd of people	a pair of shoes
a flight of steps	a suit of clothes
a flock of birds	a tribe of natives

A Write the missing words. You will find them in the list.

1. a — of people
2. a — of wolves
3. a — of grapes
4. a — of shoes
5. a — of clothes
6. a flight of —
7. a chest of —
8. a tribe of —
9. a herd of —
10. a flock of —

B Write the word which will fill each gap.

1. A — of steps led to the cabin.
2. A large — of starlings flew over the town.
3. Our milk comes from a — of Jersey cows.
4. A pack of — went hunting in the forest.
5. The hunters met a friendly — of Indians.
6. A — of people gathered to welcome the Prince.
7. The clothes were kept in an old — of drawers.
8. She bought a new — of shoes for the wedding.
9. Father gave his old — of clothes to a tramp.
10. When my aunt was in hospital my uncle took her a lovely — of black grapes.

Tom Thumb

The woodman took his family into a very thick wood where they could not see one another ten paces off. The woodman began to cut some wood, and the children to gather up the sticks and to make them into bundles. Their father and mother, seeing them all so busy, crept away from them bit by bit, and then all at once ran away through the bushes.

When the children saw that they had been left alone they started to cry loudly. Tom Thumb let them cry, for he had taken care to drop all along the road the little white stones he had in his pockets.

Then he said to them, "Do not be afraid, brothers. Father and Mother have left us here, but I will take you home again; only follow me."

They followed him, and he brought them home through the wood by the same road as they had come.

(*Tales from Perrault*)

1. Where did the woodman take his family?
2. What did he do when they got there?
3. How did the children help their father?
4. What did the father and mother do when the children were busy?
5. Why did the children start to cry?
6. Why did Tom let them cry?
7. What had Tom done on the way to the wood?
8. How was Tom able to take his brothers home again?

Group Names

The **robin** is a **bird**. So is the **sparrow** and so is the **thrush**.

They all belong to the same **group—birds**.

animals	dogs	colours	days	fish
flowers	fruits	insects	tools	trees

A Use a group name from the list above to finish each sentence.

1. Oak, ash, birch and elm are all —.
2. Terrier, corgi, spaniel and collie are all — .
3. Hammer, saw, pincers and chisel are all —.
4. Monday, Thursday, Friday and Tuesday are all —.
5. Herring, cod, hake and haddock are all —.
6. Fly, wasp, bee and gnat are all —.
7. Lion, tiger, bear and wolf are all —.
8. Red, blue, yellow and green are all —.
9. Rose, lily, tulip and crocus are all —.
10. Pear, apple, plum and banana are all —.

B In each line below there is one word which does not belong to the same group as the others. Write the odd word.

1. willow; oak; birch; daffodil; beech
2. blue; bright; black; yellow; green
3. apple; orange; turnip; lemon; pear
4. cow; goat; sheep; moth; horse
5. Christmas; Friday; Wednesday; Monday; Thursday
6. violet; dandelion; bluebell; mushroom; snowdrop

People Who Work

A Write a list of words, numbered from 1 to 10, naming these workers.

cobbler farmer porter sailor fishmonger
fireman teacher guard soldier hairdresser

B Write the missing words.

1. I asked the ⎯ when my shoes would be ready.
2. The ⎯ had some fine fillets of hake.
3. The ⎯ is giving an arithmetic lesson.
4. The ⎯ wheeled Mother's trunk to the luggage van.
5. Jane has gone to the ⎯ to have her hair cut.
6. The ⎯ blew his whistle and the train moved off.
7. The ⎯ went aboard the battleship.
8. We watched the ⎯ cutting the hay.
9. The ⎯ on sentry duty carried a rifle.
10. A big crowd saw the ⎯ rescue the boy from the burning house.

The Doers of Actions

The person who **teaches** you is your **teacher**.

Teach is the action.

Teacher is the **doer** of the action.

A Add **-er** to each of these verbs to make the name of the doer.

1. help
2. jump
3. lead
4. bowl
5. read
6. sleep
7. clean
8. dream

B Before adding **-er** to these words, double the last letter.

1. run
2. rob
3. shop
4. win
5. drum
6. swim
7. trap
8. travel

C Drop the **e** when you add **-er** to these words.

1. ride
2. dance
3. drive
4. smoke
5. make
6. lodge
7. strike
8. write

D Change **y** to **i** before adding **-er**.

1. cry
2. fly
3. dry
4. copy
5. carry
6. supply

E Write the words which fill the spaces.

1. Andrew was a strong —. (**swim**)
2. The — rang his bell then read the notice. (**cry**)
3. Every child should try to be a good —. (**read**)
4. The — was given a gold medal. (**win**)
5. He has been a — at that house for ten years. (**lodge**)
6. The — sent two parcels to the school. (**supply**)
7. Our — keeps the school very tidy. (**clean**)
8. A policeman stopped the — of the sports car. (**drive**)

Male and Female

A **boy** is a **he**, or a **male**.   A **man** is a **he**, or a **male**.

A **girl** is a **she**, or a **female**.   A **woman** is a **she**, or a **female**.

Male	Female	Male	Female
actor	actress	master	mistress
cockerel	hen	prince	princess
dog	bitch	son	daughter
gander	goose	tiger	tigress
grandfather	grandmother	waiter	waitress

A Copy these columns, then write the missing words.

Male	Female	Male	Female
1. *prince*	princess	6. *dog*	bitch
2. grandfather	*grandmother*	7. *tiger*	tigress
3. *son*	daughter	8. *actor*	actress
4. waiter	*waitress*	9. cockerel	*hen*
5. gander	*goose*	10. *master*	mistress

B Change **male** nouns to **female**, and **female** to **male**.

1. The waitress took our order and left.
2. The poodle was a dog ten months old.
3. The goose hissed at the children.
4. The master of the house was out.
5. The teacher's son was very ill.
6. The hunter shot the huge tiger.
7. The old hen scratched in the earth for worms.
8. In the evening the prince walked in the garden.

Animals

A Write the names of these animals in the order shown.

B Write the word which will complete each sentence.

bear	lion	donkey	hedgehog	kangaroo
fox	camel	giraffe	elephant	squirrel

1. The — is covered with sharp spines and can roll itself into a ball when attacked.
2. The — has a long trunk and strong tusks.
3. The — has a hump on its back and can carry people and goods across the desert.
4. The — has a spotted skin and a very long neck.
5. The — has a bushy tail which curls over its back.
6. The — is a cunning animal which steals poultry.
7. The — is called The King of Beasts. Its loud roar frightens many animals.
8. The — is a stubborn animal with very long ears. It is sometimes called an ass.
9. The — has strong hind legs which enable it to move forward in great leaps measuring as much as ten yards.
10. A — has a shaggy coat and strong claws. It can hug a person to death.

The Fox and the Goat

While reaching down to drink the water in a well one day, a fox fell in. Try as he would, he could not get out again because the walls of the well were too high.

Not long after, a goat came along. Seeing the fox down there, he asked him the reason why.

"I am enjoying the cool, pure water," replied the fox. "Wouldn't you like to jump down and taste it?"

Without stopping to think, the foolish old goat jumped down. No sooner had he reached the bottom than the cunning old fox leaped on to his back and scrambled to the top.

Looking down at the unhappy goat the fox laughed and said, "Next time, friend goat, be sure to look before you leap."

(*Aesop's Fables*)

1. What did the fox have to do before he could drink the water in the well?
2. What happened to him while he was doing this?
3. Why could he not get out of the well?
4. What did the goat ask the fox?
5. What was the answer given by the fox?
6. What did the goat do when the fox asked him to try the water?
7. How did the fox get to the top again?
8. What did he tell the goat to do the next time?

Adverbs

Andrew tiptoed **quietly** from the room.

The word **quietly** tells how he left the room.

This word is formed by adding **-ly** to quiet.

A Add **-ly** to each of these words.

quick	sad	safe	quiet	bold
calm	fond	neat	proud	kind

B When **-ly** is added to words ending with **y**, this letter is first changed to **i**.

Examples: clumsy – clumsily   hasty – hastily

Add **-ly** to these words.

easy	sleepy	lucky	angry	greedy
busy	noisy	heavy	steady	hungry

C The word which fills each space below is formed by adding **-ly** to the word in brackets. Write the ten words.

1. The flames spread so — that the house was soon burnt to the ground. (**quick**)
2. All the boys were working —. (**busy**)
3. The ship arrived — after a stormy voyage. (**safe**)
4. The snail crept — along the garden path. (**slow**)
5. The old man nodded his head —. (**sleepy**)
6. It is raining too — for you to go out. (**heavy**)
7. The young mother looked — at her baby. (**proud**)
8. Sandra wrote the letter very —. (**neat**)
9. Philip jumped over the wall quite —. (**easy**)
10. The keeper went — into the lion's cage. (**bold**)

Opposites (Change of Word)

Learn this list of opposites, then answer the questions.

back . . . front	bitter . . . sweet	break . . . mend
buy . . . . sell	dark . . . . light	fast . . . . . slow
glad . . . sorry	long . . . . short	noisy . . . quiet
	poor . . . . rich	

A Use the opposite of the word in brackets to fill each space.

Example: 1. a fast train

1. a — train (**slow**)
2. to — a rabbit (**buy**) *Sell*
3. a — room (**dark**) *bright*
4. a — seat (**back**) *front*
5. a — story (**long**) *Short*
6. a — orange (**sweet**) *sour*
7. a — street (**quiet**) *nosy*
8. a — man (**poor**) *rich*
9. to — a toy (**break**) *mend*
10. to be — (**glad**) *sad*

B Fill each gap with the opposite of the word in heavy type.

1. If the children — *brack* their toys their father will **mend** them.
2. We are going to paint both the **front** and the — *back* of our house.
3. He was — *glad* when his cousin came but **sorry** when he left.
4. Uncle will **sell** his old car and — *buy* a new one.
5. He tied the — *Short* length of cord to the **long** one.
6. The children were **quiet** in school but very — *nosy* outside.
7. Ten years ago he was —. *poor* Now he is very **rich**.
8. He wore a **dark** grey suit and a — *Light* grey hat.
9. The clock was five minutes **fast** yesterday but it is — *Slow* today.
10. The pills were — *sour* but the cough mixture was **sweet**.

Group Names

An apple is **a fruit.**   A trout is **a fish.**   A fly is an **insect.**   A doll is **a toy.**

bird	toy	tool	flower	animal
fish	tree	fruit	insect	vegetable

A Write the group name for each of these objects.

1. A rattle is a ——.
2. A peach is a ——.
3. A herring is a ——.
4. An oak is a ——.
5. A tiger is an ——.

6. A wasp is an ——.
7. A turnip is a ——.
8. A crocus is a ——.
9. A sparrow is a ——.
10. A hammer is a ——.

B Draw four columns in your book, like these. Then put the words below in their correct columns.

Fruits	Fishes	Vegetables	Tools

1. parsnip
2. rake
3. orange
4. carrot
5. herring

6. cabbage
7. lemon
8. plaice
9. spade
10. apricot

11. trowel
12. mackerel
13. beetroot
14. banana
15. spanner

16. plum
17. salmon
18. onion
19. hatchet
20. hake

Food and Drink

Copy these sentences. Use the words given to fill the spaces.

bacon	cereals	margarine	pork
beef	cream	marmalade	pudding
butter	eggs	milk	sugar
breakfast	flour	mutton	wheat

A
1. Bread, buns and cakes are made from —.
2. Flour is a fine meal or powder made from —.
3. Many children have cornflakes, puffed wheat and similar foods for —.
4. Such foods are known as —.
5. The — we eat are laid by hens.
6. Butter, eggs and sugar are used with rice to make a rice —.
7. Fruit is boiled with — to make jam.
8. Jam made with oranges is called —.

B
1. The — which we drink comes from the cow.
2. If milk is allowed to stand the — rises to the top.
3. The — which we spread on our bread is made from milk.
4. Many housewives use — instead of butter.
5. The meat we get from the cow is called —.
6. The meat from a pig is known as —.
7. — is the meat we get from the sheep.
8. — is the flesh of a pig salted and sometimes smoked.

Alphabetical Order

All these words begin with a different letter.

fruit year march board shade

To put them in **a-b-c** or alphabetical order we look at the first letter only.

board fruit march shade year

All these words begin with the same letter.

bead **b**lack **b**rick **b**ook **b**ath

To put them in alphabetical order we must look at the **second** letter in each.

    e **l** **r** **o** **a**

Now it is easy to put them in their right order.

b**a**th b**e**ad b**l**ack b**o**ok b**r**ick

A Write in alphabetical order.

1. bank	bend	boat	bite	burn
2. crop	club	case	chop	cost
3. loaf	lick	lump	lamb	leaf
4. peck	part	port	pure	pint
5. slot	scar	ship	stop	safe
6. much	mile	meat	mask	more

B Can you spot the word which is **out of order** in each of these lines?

1. nail	near	nice	nurse	noon
2. gate	glad	give	gone	grow
3. feel	fine	from	flat	fuss
4. echo	east	edge	else	even
5. pill	plan	pray	post	punt

Making Butter

One day in the summer holidays Jane went to see her Aunt Ann, who lives at Willow Farm. Jane enjoyed looking at the animals, but what she liked most was to see the butter being made.

In a cool, clean room called a dairy there were some large shallow pans holding milk. These had been left there for the cream to rise to the top. It is from the cream that the butter is made.

Aunt Ann showed Jane the churn in which butter is made. It was a kind of wooden barrel resting on a stand. At one end was a handle which turns the churn round and round.

When Aunt Ann had skimmed the cream off the milk she put it in the churn and started to turn it. After a long time she opened the churn and looked inside. Jane saw that the white cream had changed into yellow butter. She also saw the buttermilk, which is the watery part of cream. Next, the butter was washed and pressed to get the buttermilk out, and Aunt Ann put salt with it to keep it fresh. When she had made it into round pats it was ready. Aunt Ann gave Jane a pat to take home.

1. What did Jane like most at Willow Farm?
2. In which room was the butter made?
3. Why was the milk put into large shallow pans?
4. In what was the butter made?
5. What did Aunt Ann do after putting the cream in the churn?
6. What is the watery part of cream called?
7. Why did Aunt Ann wash and press the butter?
8. Why was salt added to the butter?

Verbs (Past Time)

Present Time: We **begin** our holidays today.
Past Time: They **began** their holidays yesterday.

Learn the verbs in this list, then answer the questions.

Present	Past	Present	Past	Present	Past
blow	blew	eat	ate	know	knew
break	broke	feel	felt	sleep	slept
do	did	fly	flew	take	took
drive	drove	hide	hid	tear	tore

A Copy these columns. Fill the blanks.

Present	Past	Present	Past	Present	Past
1. tear	—	5. —	took	9. fly	—
2. break	—	6. —	hid	10. —	blew
3. sleep	—	7. —	drove	11. do	—
4. know	—	8. —	ate	12 —	felt

B Write the words which must be used to fill the gaps.

1. Peter — a long time to do his sums.
2. Mr. Bond — the car into the garage.
3. I went to bed early and — all night.
4. The high wind — the leaves off the trees.
5. Barbara — a plate when she washed the dishes.
6. The dog — all his food and begged for more.
7. The lark — up into the sky.
8. James — a pain in his side.
9. Martin — the answer to every question.
10. Anne — her skirt on a rusty nail.

Birthdays

A Read this poem, then answer the questions.

> Monday's child is fair of face,
> Tuesday's child is full of grace,
> Wednesday's child is full of woe,
> Thursday's child has far to go,
> Friday's child is loving and giving,
> Saturday's child works hard for its living,
> But the child that is born on the Sabbath Day
> Is fair and wise and good and gay.

1. Which child has to work hard for a living?
2. The child born on a Tuesday is full of —.
3. Which child will be a sad child?
4. Which child will be a pretty child?
5. Which child is loving and giving?
6. Which child will travel a lot?
7. On which day is it best to be born?

B Write the names of the days of the week in order.

Opposite each day write a sentence about something you do on that day.

Examples: **Monday.** I take money to school to pay for my dinners for the week.

Tuesday. I borrow a book from the class library.

Saturday. I go shopping with Mother.

Same Sound—Different Meaning

Some words have the same sound as other words, but they differ in spelling and meaning.

Look at these four pairs of words.

Learn to spell each word. Learn the meaning of each.

hear	You **hear** with your ears.
here	I will wait **here** for you. (*in this place*)
main	The **main** road is the most important one.
mane	The long hair on the neck of a horse or a lion is called a **mane**.
meat	The flesh of an animal used for food.
meet	When people **meet** they get together.
pail	A **pail** is a kind of bucket.
pale	A **pale** person has little colour.

Write the word which will complete each sentence.

1. She looked very — after her illness. (**pail; pale**)
2. The — was too tough to eat. (**meat; meet**)
3. We did not — the postman knocking. (**here; hear**)
4. The school is on the — road. (**main; mane**)
5. The — was half full of water. (**pail; pale**)
6. The horse had a very long —. (**main; mane**)
7. I would like to live —. (**here; hear**)
8. We will — you outside the cinema. (**meat; meet**)

The Months of the Year

JANUARY	FEBRUARY	MARCH	APRIL
S . . 6 13 20 27	S . 3 10 17 24 ..	S . 2 9 16 23 30	S . . 6 13 20 27
M . . 7 14 21 28	M . 4 11 18 25 ..	M . 3 10 17 24 31	M . . 7 14 21 28
T . 1 8 15 22 29	T . 5 12 19 26 ..	T . 4 11 18 25 ..	T . 1 8 15 22 29
W . 2 9 16 23 30	W . 6 13 20 27 ..	W . 5 12 19 26 ..	W . 2 9 16 23 30
Th . 3 10 17 24 31	Th . 7 14 21 28 ..	Th . 6 13 20 27 ..	Th . 3 10 17 24 ..
F . 4 11 18 25 ..	F 1 8 15 22 29 ..	F . 7 14 21 28 ..	F . 4 11 18 25 ..
S . 5 12 19 26 ..	S 2 9 16 23	S 1 8 15 22 29 ..	S . 5 12 19 26 ..

MAY	JUNE	JULY	AUGUST
S . . 4 11 18 25	S . 1 8 15 22 29	S . . 6 13 20 27	S . 3 10 17 24 31
M . . 5 12 19 26	M . 2 9 16 23 30	M . . 7 14 21 28	M . 4 11 18 25 ..
T . . 6 13 20 27	T . 3 10 17 24 ..	T . 1 8 15 22 29	T . 5 12 19 26 ..
W . . 7 14 21 28	W . 4 11 18 25 ..	W . 2 9 16 23 30	W . 6 13 20 27 ..
Th . 1 8 15 22 29	Th . 5 12 19 26 ..	Th . 3 10 17 24 31	Th . 7 14 21 28 ..
F . 2 9 16 23 30	F . 6 13 20 27 ..	F . 4 11 18 25 ..	F 1 8 15 22 29 ..
S . 3 10 17 24 31	S . 7 14 21 28 ..	S . 5 12 19 26 ..	S 2 9 16 23 30 ..

SEPTEMBER	OCTOBER	NOVEMBER	DECEMBER
S . . 7 14 21 28	S . . 5 12 19 26	S . 2 9 16 23 30	S . . 7 14 21 28
M . 1 8 15 22 29	M . . 6 13 20 27	M . 3 10 17 24 ..	M . 1 8 15 22 29
T . 2 9 16 23 30	T . . 7 14 21 28	T . 4 11 18 25 ..	T . 2 9 16 23 30
W . 3 10 17 24 ..	W . 1 8 15 22 29	W . 5 12 19 26 ..	W . 3 10 17 24 31
Th . 4 11 18 25 ..	Th . 2 9 16 23 30	Th . 6 13 20 27 ..	Th . 4 11 18 25 ..
F . 5 12 19 26 ..	F . 3 10 17 24 31	F . 7 14 21 28 ..	F . 5 12 19 26 ..
S . 6 13 20 27 ..	S . 4 11 18 25 ..	S 1 8 15 22 29 ..	S . 6 13 20 27 ..

A Look at the calendar. Answer the questions.

1. How many months are there in the year?
2. Which month has the shortest name?
3. Write the names of the three months ending with **-ember**.
4. Which month has the longest name?
5. Which month has fewest days?
6. In which month does your birthday come?
7. Name the month in which Christmas comes.
8. Write the names of the four months which have no letter **r** in them.

B We can write the names of the months in a short way.

Copy these short forms and learn them.

1. January......Jan.
2. February ....Feb.
3. March.......Mar.
4. April........April
5. May ....May
6. June ....June
7. July ....July
8. August ....Aug.
9. September .....Sept.
10. October ....Oct.
11. November .....Nov.
12. December .....Dec.

Writing Dates

| **1st** | **21st** | **31st** | Write **st** after |
| first | twenty-first | thirty-first | the number. |

| **2nd** | **22nd** | Write **nd** after the number. |
| second | twenty-second | |

| **3rd** | **23rd** | Write **rd** after the number. |
| third | twenty-third | |

For all other numbers in the calendar add **th**.

| **4th** | **11th** | **17th** | **25th** |
| fourth | eleventh | seventeenth | twenty-fifth |

A Use numbers to write these.

1. fifth
2. tenth
3. second
4. first
5. sixth

6. third
7. ninth
8. twenty-first
9. sixteenth
10. fourth

11. thirty-first
12. seventh
13. twenty-third
14. twelfth
15. twenty-second

B **Writing Dates:** 14th May or May 14th

1. Write the date for the twenty-fourth of September.
2. On which date does New Year's Day come?
3. What is the date today?
4. Write the date of your birthday.
5. Write the date for August the twenty-first.
6. On which date does Christmas Day come?

A Camping Holiday

Last summer Roger Dunne and his sister Jill spent a most enjoyable camping holiday in Wales with their father and mother. Their new blue tent, which had two bedrooms and a living-room, was pitched in a large field near a sandy bay. There were many other tents of all sizes, shapes and colours.

Early every morning the two children and their father went bathing, while their mother prepared the breakfast. When breakfast was over, and the washing-up done, they all went down to the beach and played cricket. But Mrs. Dunne always left early to get the lunch ready by one o'clock.

In the afternoons the parents sat on the sand reading, while the children went fishing with their nets in the clear pools among the rocks. For their evening meal they all went to a farmhouse at the foot of the hill, and stayed chatting to the farmer and his wife long after the meal was over. At sunset they strolled back to their tent, tucked themselves up snugly in their sleeping-bags and slept soundly until they were woken next morning by the songs of the birds.

1. What kind of holiday did Roger and Jill have last summer?
2. Where did they pitch their tent?
3. How many rooms did their tent have?
4. What did the children and their father do while their mother was preparing breakfast?
5. How did the children spend the afternoons?
6. Where did the family have their evening meal?
7. What did they do after returning to their tent at sunset?
8. What awakened them in the morning?

Rhymes

A Read this poem carefully. Then copy it, putting in the words which you think will end each line.

Twinkle, twinkle, little (car; star; bar; tar),
How I wonder what you (far; jar; are; war)!
Up above the world so (lie; nigh; shy; high)
Like a diamond in the (sly; pie; sky; sty).

When the blazing sun is (let; set; bet; net),
And the grass with dew is (pet; met; wet; yet),
Then you show your little (tight; fight; sight; light),
Twinkle, twinkle, all the (right; night; might; white).

B Write the list of words in capital letters. After each word write the three words in small letters which will rhyme with it.

Example: 1. LATE   gate, weight, wait

1. LATE	mend	park	stout
2. BARK	gate	pout	sing
3. OUT	cling	weight	lend
4. BEND	mark	about	bring
5. RING	wait	lark	send

C The missing word in each line below rhymes with the word in capitals.

1. CRAWL   Two pence is a — sum of money.
2. HEAT   I will — you at the corner of the street.
3. NAIL   The cakes were too — to eat.
4. THESE   If you — a dog he may bite you.
5. SNORE   Mother asked Sally to — the tea.

Compound Words

A **compound** word is formed by joining together two or more words.

Example: **tea + pot = teapot**

A Write the name of each object. Show the two words which make up each compound word.

Example: 1. **rail + way = railway**

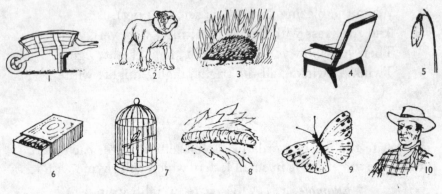

| armchair | birdcage | butterfly | cowboy | hedgehog |
| wheelbarrow | matchbox | silkworm | bulldog | snowdrop |

B In each line below, join together the two words in heavy type to form a compound word. Start with the second word.

1. a **fish** which is **gold** in colour
2. a **ship** which is driven by **steam**
3. a **stand** on which a **band** plays
4. a **cloth** which covers a **table**
5. a **ball** made of **snow**
6. a **room** for a **bed**
7. **weed** which grows in the **sea**
8. a **tray** to hold cigarette **ash**
9. a **box** for keeping **cash**
10. a **coat** which is worn **over** all other clothes

The Long and the Short

There is a short way of writing some words.

Avenue ....Ave.	Road ....Rd.
Doctor.....Dr.	Square......Sq.
Missis .....Mrs.	Street.......St.
Mister .....Mr.	Terrace .....Terr.

A Write each of these the short way:

1. Doctor Smith
2. High Street
3. Mister Lee
4. Station Terrace
5. Missis Bond
6. Bush Avenue
7. Victoria Square
8. Redlands Road

Initials

Instead of writing a person's Christian name or names in full we write only the **first letter,** as a **capital**, followed by a full stop.

Examples: Edward Marsh   Arthur John Bond
            E. Marsh   A. J. Bond

B Draw envelopes in your exercise book and write these names and addresses, using initials and the short forms you have learnt.

1. Mister Ronald Green, of 12 Church Street, Camford.
2. Missis Jane Everson, of 9 Norton Road, Benham.
3. Miss Eva May Brent, of 16 Park Terrace, Broxley.
4. Doctor David Alan Johnson, of 23 Poplar Avenue, Reddington.
5. Mister William Frederick Dixon, of 31 Chester Square, Podworth.

Short Forms

The short way of writing **has not** is **hasn't**.
We can also write **that is** a short way — **that's**.

In a similar way the word **will** can be added to words and written in a short way.

I will	you will	he will
I'll	you'll	he'll
she will	we will	they will
she'll	we'll	they'll

Remember that the **'** shows that the letters **wi** have been left out.

A Write the short form for:

1. is not
2. we will
3. here is
4. he will
5. are not

6. do not
7. where is
8. you will
9. did not
10. they will

11. I will
12. does not
13. it is
14. she will
15. what is

B Write the short form of the two words in heavy type in these sentences.

1. I know **you will** be pleased with your present.
2. Peter says **there is** plenty of time.
3. Next time **we will** go by train.
4. We must find out **who is** going to the party.
5. I promise you **I will** do my best.
6. If Barbara is late **she will** be scolded.
7. The boys said **they will** call on their way home.
8. Alan **would not** get up when called.
9. Very likely **he will** be late for school.
10. Everybody says **it is** a fine drawing.

Similars

A **plucky** sailor   A **brave** sailor

The words **plucky** and **brave** are similar in meaning.

Learn the list of similars, then answer the questions.

aged . . . . . . old	cash . . . . money
connect . . . join	garments . . . . clothes
glance . . . . . look	handsome . . . beautiful
loiter . . . . . linger	plump . . . . . . fat
slender . . . . slim	tremble . . . . . shake

A For each word in heavy type give a word which has a similar meaning.

1. The **cash** was taken to the bank.
2. The plumber came to **connect** the pipes.
3. He is a very **handsome** child.
4. The Browns had a **plump** goose for Christmas.
5. You should not **loiter** on the way home.
6. He did not even **glance** at the book.
7. The dancer had a **slender** figure.
8. The door was opened by an **aged** servant.
9. The trains made the old bridge **tremble**.
10. All **garments** sold in this shop are tailor made.

B Write simpler words which are similar in meaning to these. Some you learnt in Book 1.

1. broad	5. repair	9. commence	13. correct
2. plucky	6. collect	10. reply	14. peril
3. finish	7. difficult	11. wealthy	15. assist
4. large	8. stout	12. weeping	16. farewell

Mr. Cherry

Once upon a time there was a piece of wood. It was not the best wood, but just a common piece, such as we use to light a fire.

One day this piece of wood happened to be in the shop of an old carpenter whose name was Mr. Antonio, but everyone called him Mr. Cherry, because the end of his nose was always red and shiny like a cherry.

As soon as Mr. Cherry saw this piece of wood he rubbed his hands together for joy, and said to himself:

"This has come in the nick of time; it is just what I want to make a leg for my little table."

He took his sharp hatchet and was just going to strip off the bark and trim it into shape. But just as he raised the hatchet to strike the first blow he paused with his hand in the air, for he heard a tiny, tiny voice which said warningly:

"Don't strike me too hard!"

1. What kind of wood was it?
2. What was the real name of the carpenter?
3. By what name did everyone call him?
4. Why did they give him this name?
5. How did the carpenter feel when he saw the piece of wood?
6. What did he intend to make out of it?
7. What was he going to use his sharp hatchet for?
8. Why did he pause with his hand in the air just as he was going to strike the first blow?

Fun With Words

In each of the lines of words below there are two pairs of words and one odd word.

You have to find the word which will make up the third pair.

Look at the first pair of words in line 1. **ten, tent**

The second word is made by writing the letter **t** after the first word.

Look at the second pair. The second word is again formed by writing **t** after the first word. **sea, seat**

To find the missing word write **t** after the odd word.
star, start

A Now find the other missing words. In each line a different letter must be added.

1. ten, tent   sea, seat   star, —
2. pan, pane   hop, hope   hid, —
3. bun, bung   ran, rang   thin, —
4. ten, tend   ban, band   win, —
5. tea, team   for, form   war, —

B From the letters in the word TENS we can make the word NEST.

From the letters in the words in capitals make words which will fit into the spaces below.

1. TENS   There were five eggs in the —.
2. MEAT   The performing bear was quite —.
3. OWLS   The journey was a very — one.
4. DARE   Every child should learn to — well.
5. RACE   We should take great — with our spelling.

More Fun With Words

A Each star in these sentences stands for a letter.
Each group of letters spells a word.

Example: 1. Mary has long g***en hair.
The missing letters are **old**.

Each missing word has **three** letters. Write the missing words only.

1. Mary has long g***en hair.
2. The plants were bl*** down by the strong wind.
3. Pigs g***t when they eat their food.
4. The little boy sat down on the three-legged s***l.
5. We sometimes have snow in the ***ter.
6. Wolves were h***ing in the forest.
7. The ***tain of the ship was a Dane.
8. The mon*** hung from the tree by his long tail.

B Each missing word has **four** letters. Write the missing words only.

1. Wendy's class will have a new t****er next term.
2. Bees had s****ed on an apple tree in the garden.
3. The tired horse was taken to the st****.
4. Mother lit the fire because the room was c****y.
5. Paul uses b****s to keep his trousers up.
6. The engine was letting off s****.
7. We saw the p**** landing on the runway.
8. The express t**** ran off the rails.

Verbs (Past Time)

Present Time: I **feel** a pain in my side today.

Past Time: I **felt** a pain in my side yesterday.

Learn the words in this list, then answer the questions.

Present	Past	Present	Past
build . . . . . . built		rise . . . . rose
creep . . . . . . crept		see . . . . saw
grow . . . . grew		sink . . . . sank
ride . . . . rode		speak . . . . . . spoke
ring . . . . rang		steal . . . . stole

A Copy these columns. Fill the blanks.

Present	Past	Present	Past
1. —	saw	6. speak	—
2. —	rang	7. steal	—
3. —	rose	8. ride	—
4. —	grew	9. build	—
5. —	sank	10. creep	—

B Write the words which will fill the gaps.

1. He — to the seaside on his new bicycle.
2. The boat filled with water and —.
3. The boy — the school bell.
4. The gardener — some beautiful roses.
5. I — to him on the telephone.
6. The boys — a sand castle on the beach.
7. We — two bear cubs in the zoo.
8. The thief — the money from the till.
9. I — at seven o'clock yesterday morning.
10. The burglar — quietly into the house.

Using TOOK and TAKEN

I **took** a book home.

I **have taken** a book home. (**have** helps the word **taken**)

The book **was taken** home. (**was** helps the word **taken**)

The word **took** needs no helping word.

The word **taken** always has a helping word.

is taken	are taken	has taken	had taken
was taken	were taken	have taken	will be taken

A Use **took** or **taken** to fill each space.

1. It was —
2. You —
3. He has —
4. I —
5. They are —
6. You have —
7. He —
8. We were —
9. It will be —
10. She —

B Fill each space with **took** or **taken**.

1. The man was — ill at the football match.
2. They — the man to the hospital.
3. Susan — her doll to bed with her.
4. She — two pills after dinner.
5. The thief — all the money in the house.
6. Jean has — great care with her work.
7. The two men were — to prison.
8. After Alan had — his shoes to the shoe repairer he went fishing.
9. As it was raining father — his umbrella.
10. The dustmen have — the rubbish away.

When People Speak

Look at this sentence:

"This orange is sour," said Robert.

The words spoken by Robert were **This orange is sour**.
Notice that these words are inside the " and ".
The first commas come before the first word spoken.
"This . . .
The last commas come just after the last word spoken.
. . . sour,"

Notice that the " come after the ,

. . . sour",	. . . sour",	. . . sour,"
wrong	**wrong**	**right**

The last commas also come after a question mark.

A Copy these sentences. Put in the " and ".

1. Pass me the broom, please, said Mrs. Norland.
2. Are you tired? asked the teacher.
3. I can see you, shouted Brian.
4. Please, Mummy, may I have an apple? begged Simon.
5. Come here, Spot, said the little boy to his dog.
6. I don't want to go to bed yet, said Sandra with a pout.
7. Hurry up, Linda, or you'll be late, said her mother.
8. Spare a penny for the guy, please? asked the two boys.
9. Here is five pence for you, replied the gentleman.
10. Be quiet, baby's sleeping, whispered Jennifer's mother.

B Write three sentences of your own in which there are words spoken by people.

John and the Cherries

One day John went shopping with his mother. Their first call was at the fruiterer's, and while his mother was buying the fruit John looked longingly at a basket containing lovely red cherries.

"Help yourself to a handful, John," said the fruiterer, but John did not move.

"I'm sure you like cherries, don't you?" asked the puzzled shopkeeper, and John nodded his head quickly. Thinking that the boy was too shy to help himself the fruiterer went to the basket and gave John a large handful.

When they had left the shop John's mother asked him why he had not taken the cherries when the fruiterer had told him to.

"Well, you see Mummy," replied John, "his hand is twice as big as mine."

1. At what shop did John and his mother call first?
2. What was John doing while his mother was buying the fruit?
3. What did the fruiterer tell John to do?
4. Did John do as he was told?
5. What did the fruiterer do when he saw John was so shy?
6. What did John's mother ask him after they had left the shop?
7. What was John's reply?

Write the Missing Words

A

1. A sheep is covered with —.
   A rabbit is covered with —.

2. A young cat is called a —.
   A young dog is called a —.

3. A dog barks.
   A lion —.

4. The meat from a cow is called —.
   The meat from a pig is called —.

5. A bus travels on land.
   A ship travels on —.

6. Mr. is a short way of writing Mister.
   Dr. is a short way of writing —.

7. You see with your eyes.
   You smell with your —.

8. Your foot is at the end of your —.
   Your hand is at the end of your —.

B We can put these pairs of questions in a different way.

For the first pair we can write:

> Sheep is to **wool** as **rabbit** is to —.

The answer is **fur**, as you already know.

Now write the missing words.

1. **Cat** is to **kitten** as **dog** is to —.
2. **Dog** is to **bark** as **lion** is to —.
3. **Cow** is to **beef** as **pig** is to —.
4. **Ship** is to **sea** as **bus** is to —.
5. **Mr.** is to **Mister** as **Dr.** is to —.
6. **See** is to **eyes** as **smell** is to —.
7. **Foot** is to **leg** as **hand** is to —.

Pictures and Sentences

Write a sentence about each picture.
Some of the words are given to help you.

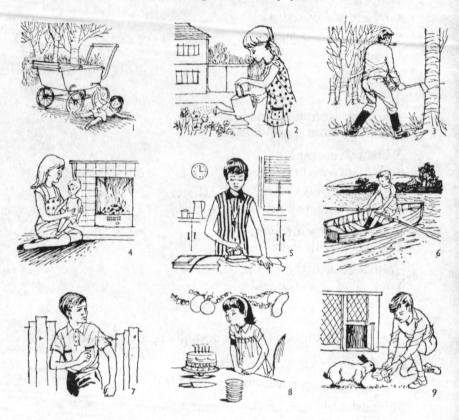

1. . . . doll . . . fell . . . pram . . . ground.
2. . . . girl . . . watering . . . flowers . . . garden.
3. . . . man . . . cutting . . . tree . . . axe.
4. Ann . . . sitting . . . floor . . . nursing . . .
5. Jane . . . ironing . . . clothes . . . board.
6. Peter . . . rowing . . . boat . . . towards . . .
7. . . . tore . . . shirt . . . nail . . . fence.
8. Carol . . . blowing . . . candles . . . birthday . . .
9. . . . giving . . . rabbit . . . leaf . . . lettuce.

Telling the Time

Look at the number to which the big hand points on each clock.   Learn the times shown.

five minutes past   ten minutes past   twenty minutes past   twenty-five minutes past

five minutes to   ten minutes to   twenty minutes to   twenty-five minutes to

Each of these clocks shows the time a train leaves the station. Write the name of the place to which each train is going and the time of leaving.

 1. The train to London leaves at ....

2. The Brighton train leaves at ....

 3. The Fishguard Express leaves at ....

4. The train to Chester leaves at ....

 5. The Birmingham train leaves at ....

6. The train to Torquay leaves at ....

 7. The Bristol train leaves at ....

Using the Right Verb

A Write the verb in the list which fits each space.

bandage	catch	drive	fight	learn
plant	play	roast	row	strike

1. to — a boat
2. to — meat
3. to — a car
4. to — a tree
5. to — a lesson

6. to — a cold
7. to — a game
8. to — a battle
9. to — a cut
10. to — a blow

B Choose the right word from the list to finish each sentence.

built	mounted	packed	returned	sheltered
spent	stamped	taught	thanked	warmed

1. We — from the rain in an old barn.
2. James — from his holiday yesterday.
3. The roadmen — their feet to get warm.
4. Father — me to ride a bicycle.
5. Marion has — all her money.
6. I — the parcel and gave it to Michael.
7. Sally — herself by the blazing fire.
8. The new house was — in less than six months.
9. I — Susan for the lovely present she sent me.
10. The cowboy — his horse and rode off.

C Use each pair of words in a sentence of your own.

1. poked; fire
2. sang; carol
3. darned; socks
4. burnt; toast
5. drank; tea
6. rang; bell

Where They Live

A Copy these sentences, filling each space with the name of the home of each creature.

den	web	cage	hutch	kennel
sty	nest	hive	shell	stable

1. A snail carries its home, a —, on its back.
2. The old sow and her piglets were lying down in their —.
3. Martin made a cosy — for his pet rabbit.
4. The lion was in his — playing with his cubs.
5. Black Beauty was put in a — with another horse.
6. A swarm of bees flew out of the —.
7. We watched the spider weaving its —.
8. There are now two budgerigars in the —.
9. The little terrier was fast asleep in his —.
10. There were five eggs in the robin's —.

Putting Words in Order

B Arrange the words in each sentence in their right order. Begin each sentence with a capital letter, and end it with a full stop.

1. trees oak on grow Acorns
2. the from cow get We milk
3. a flower The spring is crocus
4. called a cow is from beef meat The
5. on River London the stands Thames
6. late train an was hour My
7. is called young kitten cat a A
8. warm Eskimoes very clothes wear

Black Beauty and Ginger

My master and mistress made up their minds to pay a visit to some friends who lived about forty-six miles from our home. James was to drive them in the carriage, which was to be drawn by Ginger and me.

The first day we travelled thirty-two miles. There were some long, steep hills, but James drove so carefully that we were never tired or troubled. He never forgot to put on the brake as we went downhill, nor to take it off at the right place. He kept our feet on the smoothest part of the road; and if the uphill was very long he set the wheels a little across the road, so that the carriage should not run back, and gave us time to breathe. All these little things, together with kind words, help a horse very much.

We stopped once or twice on the road; and just as the sun was going down, we reached the town where we were to spend the night. We stopped at the biggest hotel, which was in the Market Place. We drove under an archway into a long yard, at the end of which were the stables where we were to rest.

(*Black Beauty* — by Anna Sewell)

1. What did Black Beauty's master and mistress make up their minds to do?
2. How far did they travel the first day?
3. Why were the horses never tired or troubled?
4. What did James do as they went downhill?
5. Why did James set the carriage wheels across the road when going up a long hill?
6. At what time of day did they reach the town?
7. Where did they stop?
8. Where were the stables in which the two horses were to spend the night?

Using ATE and EATEN

George **ate** his apple.

George **has eaten** his apple. (**has** helps the word **eaten**)

The apple **was eaten** by George. (**was** helps the word **eaten**)

The word **ate** needs no helping word.

The word **eaten** always has a helping word, like **has** eaten, **have** eaten, **is** eaten, **are** eaten, **was** eaten, **were** eaten, **had** eaten, and so on.

A Use **ate** or **eaten** to fill each space.

1. I —
2. You have —
3. It was —
4. He —
5. You —
6. He has —
7. We —
8. They are —
9. She —
10. We had —

B Fill each space with **ate** or **eaten**.

1. John — his supper and went to bed.
2. After John had — his supper he went to bed.
3. Many meals are — on the beach in summer.
4. The monkey — all the nuts the children gave him.
5. The jumper was — by moths.
6. The little bear's porridge had been — by Goldilocks.
7. The puppy — his food and looked for more.
8. When you have — your food you may leave the table.
9. Ian — the lean meat and left the fat.
10. Bread is — all over the world.

Rhymes

The last word has been left out of each line in this poem.
You will find these rhyming words in the list below.

A Copy the poem, filling in the missing words.

| mouse | eyes | day | hall | quays | noon |
| house | rise | way | wall | trees | moon |

The Moon

The moon has a face like the clock in the —;
She shines on thieves on the garden —,
On streets and fields and harbour —,
And birdies asleep in the forks of —.

The squalling cat and the squeaking —,
The howling dog by the door of the —,
The bat that lies in bed at —,
All love to be out by the light of the —.

But all of the things that belong to the —
Cuddle to sleep to be out of her —;
And flowers and children close their —
Till up in the morning the sun shall —.

B After each of the words in heavy type write three other words which rhyme with it.

The first letters are given to help you.

1. **bat**	r . .	h . .	p . .
2. **lard**	c . . .	y . . .	h . . .
3. **tack**	r . . .	bl . . .	st . . .
4. **and**	h . . .	br . . .	gr . . .
5. **bag**	fl . .	dr . .	st . .
6. **lick**	p . . .	tr . . .	qu . . .

Sentences

A Write the beginning of each sentence. Then choose the ending which will match it.

> *Example:* 1. The greedy boy was ill because he had eaten too much.

Beginning	Ending
1. The greedy boy was ill	father looked hot and tired.
2. It was raining heavily	The Ship of the Desert.
3. As Robert was covered with spots	in a dozen.
4. After mowing the lawns	please let me know.
5. The camel is often called	and went off to school.
6. The load carried by a ship	that the ponds were frozen.
7. Paul picked up his satchel	because he had eaten too much.
8. If you want any help	his mother sent for the doctor.
9. The weather was so cold	is called a cargo.
10. There are twelve things	so Brian put on his mackintosh.

B Copy these beginnings. Add your own endings.
1. Roger burst into tears . . . .
2. Just as I left the house . . . .
3. Every Christmas Eve . . . .
4. While mother was baking cakes . . . .

C Begin each sentence in your own way.
1. . . . . a very long way from home.
2. . . . . and we were soaking wet.
3. . . . . because he felt too tired.
4. . . . . so we could not travel by car.

Forming Adjectives

Many adjectives are formed by adding **ful** to a noun.

> *Examples:* hope — hope**ful** (full of hope)
> joy   — joy**ful**   (full of joy)

Note that in adding **-full** one **l** is dropped.

> hope + full = hope**ful**
> joy   + full = joy**ful**

A Choose the adjective ending with **-ful** which will fill each gap.

beautiful	careful	harmful	helpful	painful
peaceful	playful	thankful	truthful	useful

1. a kitten which is full of play   a — kitten
2. a village in which there is peace   a — village
3. a girl of great beauty   a — girl
4. a driver who takes great care   a — driver
5. a cut which gives much pain   a — cut
6. a book which is of great use   a — book
7. a friend who gives help   a — friend
8. a person who is full of thanks   a — person
9. a boy who speaks the truth   a — boy
10. a habit which causes harm   a — habit

B Add **-ful** to each of these words. Then choose three of the words you have made and use them in sentences of your own, one word in each sentence.

1. shame   3. wonder   5. hope
2. delight   4. cheer   6. hate

Opposites (Change of Word)

Learn the list of **opposites**, then answer the questions.

always . . never	asleep . . awake	better . . . . worse
blunt . . . sharp	cruel . . . kind	evil . . . . . . good
heavy . . . light	less . . . . . more	narrow . . . wide
	pull . . . . push	

A Use the **opposite** of the word in brackets to fill each space.

Example: 1. a **blunt** knife

1. a — knife (**sharp**)
2. a — master (**kind**)
3. a — man (**evil**)
4. he was — (**asleep**)
5. — danger (**more**)
6. a — road (**narrow**)
7. a — parcel (**light**)
8. to — the door (**push**)
9. — tired (**always**)
10. a — player (**better**)

B Write the word which will fill each space.

1. You pull to open the door and — to close it.
2. The small box was quite — but the big one was heavy.
3. Do what is good. Avoid what is —.
4. At seven o'clock Pat was wide awake, but Judith was still —.
5. Always be kind to animals. They do not like — people.
6. The knife was blunt but the butcher soon made it —.
7. He always makes promises but — keeps them.
8. The road was wide in most places, but quite — in some.
9. Mary's cold was better this morning but it is — tonight.
10. The men wanted more pay and — work.

Heidi and the Goats

When supper was over Heidi's grandfather began to busy himself with some wood.

"What are you doing, Grandfather?" asked Heidi.

"Making a high stool for you," he replied.

Heidi clapped her hands with delight, and watched with great interest while the stool began to take shape.

But soon a shrill whistle was heard. It was Peter come back with the goats. Heidi rushed forward to meet him and danced about with the goats. Peter left two and then went off with the rest of the flock.

"Are these your goats, Grandfather?" asked Heidi. "What are they called?"

"The white one is Little Swan, and the brown one Little Bear," was the reply.

Heidi stroked the white goat while her grandfather milked it. Then they went inside. Heidi drank more milk from her bowl and then began to feel sleepy.

1. How did the grandfather busy himself after the meal was over?
2. What was he going to make?
3. How did Heidi show her delight?
4. What was heard while the grandfather was working?
5. What did Heidi do when she saw Peter?
6. How many goats did Peter leave for the grandfather?
7. What were the names of these goats?
8. What did Heidi do while her grandfather was milking the white goat?

Same Sound—Different Meaning

Some words have the **same sound** as other words, but there
is a **difference in spelling and in meaning**.

Look at these four pairs of words.
Learn to spell each word. Learn the meaning of each.

pain	He felt no **pain** when he had his tooth out.
pane	A new **pane** of glass was fixed in the window.
road	Many cars were parked at the side of the **road**.
rode	Ian **rode** to school on his new bicycle.
sail	One **sail** of the ship was torn by the strong wind.
sale	All goods were very cheap at the **sale**.
there	I left the dish **there**. (*in that place*)
their	The two boys had lost **their** pencils. (*belonging to them*)

Write the word which will fill the gap.

1. The children love — mother very much. (**there; their**)
2. The — was muddy after the heavy rain. (**road; rode**)
3. Mother bought the carpet at a —. (**sail; sale**)
4. Susan had a — in her arm. (**pain; pane**)
5. Alan — his pony over the fields. (**road; rode**)
6. We waited — for an hour. (**there; their**)
7. The cricket ball broke a — in the window. (**pain; pane**)
8. The — of the yacht was lowered as it reached the shore.
   (**sail; sale**)

Containers

A **purse** holds or contains **money**. A **caddy** contains **tea**. Both are called **containers**.

A Write the names of these containers. Look at the list.

bin	vase	purse	basket	scuttle
jug	cup	caddy	wallet	envelope

B Copy the sentences. Write the name of a container in each space.

1. Coal is often kept in a —.
2. Mother had no loose change in her —.
3. The — was full of rubbish.
4. Father had several pound notes in his —.
5. I drink a — of tea at eleven o'clock every morning.
6. There was no milk left in the —.
7. Our — will hold two packets of tea.
8. Many women carry their goods in a — when they are shopping.
9. David put the letter in the — and posted it.
10. There were some beautiful tulips in the glass —.

Using Longer Words

The word **where** can be joined to **any, every, no** and **some**.

> any + where = **anywhere**
> no + where = **nowhere**
> every + where = **everywhere**
> some + where = **somewhere**

A Use one of these longer words to fill each space.

1. The hammer must be — in the house.
2. We looked — for the lost hammer.
3. The hammer was — to be seen.
4. We could not find the hammer —.

The word **body** can be joined to **any, every, no** and **some**.

> any + body = **anybody**   no + body = **nobody**
> every + body = **everybody**   some + body = **somebody**

B Write the words which will fill the gaps.

1. I don't think there is — at home.
2. We should be kind to —.
3. You must get — to help you in the garden.
4. Jill knocked at the door but — answered.

The word **ever** can be joined to **when, where, who, what, how** and **which**.

C Write the **-ever** words which will finish these sentences.

1. He never wears a hat — cold the weather is.
2. People must buy food — it costs.
3. — took the money must give it back.
4. You can visit us — you like.

Joining Sentences

The word **because** can be used to join two sentences.

Example: The dog bit John. He was teasing it. (*two sentences*)
The dog bit John **because** he was teasing it. (*one sentence*)

A Use **because** to join these sentences.

1. Roy was very happy. There was a holiday.
2. He did not drink his tea. It was cold.

B Use **and** to join these sentences.

1. Peter dropped the cup. It broke.
2. Henry went into the park. He had a ride on the swing.

C Use **but** to join these sentences.

1. It was a lovely hat. It was too small for Penny.
2. We waited for Carol. She did not turn up.

D Use **so** to join these sentences.

1. The weather was bitterly cold. Colin wore gloves.
2. Robin was a naughty boy. He was sent to bed early.

E Write the missing word — **and, but, so, because** — in each sentence.

1. We were thirsty — we called at a farm for a glass of milk.
2. Michael wanted to bathe — his mother said it was too cold.
3. Mother made the cakes — put them in the oven.
4. He felt cold — he had no overcoat.
5. Margaret jumped over the stream — Mary fell in.
6. The butcher cut the meat — weighed it.
7. The train was late — of the fog.
8. Ann could not do her sums — Janet helped her.

Words With More Than One Meaning

Some words have more than one meaning.

The teacher told the children to **stand** up.

He put the umbrella in the **stand** in the hall.

Use the words in the list to fill these spaces. The same word must be used for each pair of sentences.

blind	felt	foot	last	long
mean	rock	suit	top	trunk

1. The dress is too — so I must shorten it.
   I often — for a holiday in Spain.

2. The miser was too — to buy food for himself.
   Some words — much the same as other words.

3. I think this dress will — you.
   Henry wore a navy blue — at the wedding.

4. Under the carpet was a layer of —.
   Carol — ill, so she went to bed early.

5. A — person cannot see.
   She pulled the — down over the window.

6. Mother packed the — for the holidays.
   The elephant took the bun with his long —.

7. The strip of wood was one — in length.
   He was lame because he had hurt his —.

8. The shoe repairer put the shoe on his —.
   I have warned you for the — time.

9. On the beach was a huge —.
   Jane tried to — the baby to sleep.

10. Humpty Dumpty was sitting on — of the wall.
    The pretty — was spinning round and round.

The Ducklings

From the wall which surrounded the old mansion all the way down to the water's edge grew a forest of burdock leaves. Here sat a duck upon her nest, hatching a quantity of eggs. But she was getting tired of sitting there day after day, for she seldom had any visitors. The other ducks liked better to swim about on the canals that ran through the garden than to visit her in her loneliness.

At length, however, there was a crackling in one of the eggs, then in a second, third, fourth, fifth and sixth. "Peep! peep!" sounded from here; "Peep! peep!" sounded from there, at least a dozen times. All of a sudden there was life in the eggs, and the little half-naked ducklings thrust out their heads as out of a window.

"Quick! quick!" their mother cried, so the little ones made as much haste as they could. They looked about on every side at the tall green leaves, and their mother let them look as long as they liked, for green is good for the eyes.

"How large the world is!" they said, and certainly there lay before them much more space than in their eggs.

1. What was the duck doing?
2. Why was she tired of sitting there?
3. What did the other ducks like better to do?
4. How many ducklings were hatched?
5. How did the ducklings look when they came out of their shells?
6. What did the ducklings see as they looked round them?
7. Why did the mother allow her young ones to look about as much as they liked?
8. What kind of world did the ducklings think they had come into?

Writing Sentences About Pictures

Write one sentence about each of these pictures.
The list of words will help you.

barber
branch
clipping
coming
cutting
haircut
hedge
holding
looking
monkey
raining
sewing
stable
swinging
tail
through
trimming
umbrella
water
window

Using GAVE and GIVEN

Aunt Judy **gave** Paul five pence (5p).

Aunt Judy **has given** Paul five pence (5p). (**has** helps the word **given**)

Paul **was given** five pence (5p) by Aunt Judy. (**was** helps the word **given**)

The word **gave** needs no helping word.

The word **given** always has a helping word, like **has** given, **have** given, **is** given, **are** given, **was** given, **were** given, **had** given, and so on.

A Use **gave** or **given** to fill each space.

1. He has —
2. She —
3. It was —
4. You —
5. They had —
6. We have —
7. I —
8. They have —
9. They were —
10. We —

B Write the word which fills each space.

1. The teacher — each child a new pencil.
2. Each child was — a new pencil.
3. All the pens were — out.
4. Ann has — Carol a sweet.
5. Mother — me a big red apple.
6. Much money is — to the poor every day.
7. Jennifer — her mother a kiss before going to bed.
8. Every child at the party will be — a toy.
9. Mary was sorry that she had — her doll away.
10. Colin liked the bat which Uncle Fred — him.

Things Which Are Alike

When something is very light in weight we say it is
as **light** as a **feather**.

This is because a feather is so very, very light.

Learn the sayings in this list, then write the missing words
below.

as black as pitch	as hot as fire
as brown as a berry	as soft as putty
as easy as A B C	as sour as vinegar
as green as grass	as stiff as a poker
as hard as nails	as weak as a kitten

A

1. as weak as a —
2. as sour as —
3. as easy as —
4. as hot as —
5. as brown as a —
6. as green as —
7. as hard as —
8. as stiff as a —
9. as soft as —
10. as black as —

B

1. as — as fire
2. as — as grass
3. as — as nails
4. as — as putty
5. as — as a kitten
6. as — as a poker
7. as — as A B C
8. as — as vinegar
9. as — as pitch
10. as — as a berry

C Write the missing words.

1. John felt as weak as a — after his illness.
2. The soldier held himself as stiff as a —.
3. He returned from the seaside as brown as a —.
4. The cooking apple was as — as vinegar.
5. Andrew found the sum as easy as —.

Sounds

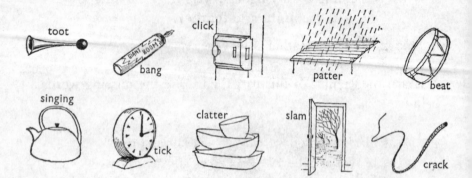

A Write the name of each sound.

1. the — of a whip
2. the — of dishes
3. the — of a drum
4. the — of a squib
5. the — of a clock
6. the — of a door
7. the — of a horn
8. the — of a kettle
9. the — of raindrops
10. the — of a lock

B Write the **sound** word which suits each sentence.

1. The — of raindrops on the window awakened the children.
2. We heard the — of drums as the soldiers drew near.
3. There was a — as the key was turned in the lock.
4. The room was so quiet that we could hear the — of the clock.
5. The — of the kettle told us that tea was nearly ready.
6. The horse jumped at the — of the whip.
7. From the kitchen came the — of dishes.
8. With a — of the door Brian left the room in a bad temper.
9. The car went past with a — of the horn.
10. The squib went off with a loud —.

Using Adjectives

    1. The man walked down the road.

    2. The **old** man walked down the road.

Sentence 2. is better than sentence 1. because it tells us something about the man. He was **old**.

    3. The **old** man walked down the **dusty** road.

This is better than either 1. or 2. because it also tells us something about the road. It was **dusty**.

A Copy these sentences, filling each space with a suitable adjective from the list.

angry	blazing	brave	clever	cosy
cold	damaged	delicious	foggy	frightened
hungry	kind	lovely	naughty	nearby
pretty	ripe	savage	stormy	straying

    1. The — girl wore a — dress.
    2. The — huntsman enjoyed the — dinner.
    3. A — dog was snarling at the — boy.
    4. It was a — — night.
    5. The — sailor dived into the — sea to save his mate.
    6. A — man gave William a — banana.
    7. There was a — fire in the — kitchen.
    8. The — car was towed to a — garage.
    9. The — sheepdog rounded up the — sheep.
  10. The — father punished his — son.

B Make sentences of your own from these words, putting two adjectives in each.

    1. man — won — prize
    2. baby — played — rattle
    3. sun — shone — sky

    4. ship — wrecked — shore
    5. shopkeeper — served — customer
    6. cat — chased — mouse

The Faithful Collie

James Hogg was a well-known poet, but he was also a shepherd. One night, when he was out with his sheep, it started to snow heavily. Knowing that he would have to get his flock in, Hogg whistled for his faithful collie. When she came running to him, he told her to get all the sheep in from one side of the moor while he did the same on the other side. Off they both went.

The shepherd returned much later, bringing with him the sheep he had rounded up. As there was no sign of the collie, he went into his cabin to wait.

After several hours a painful whine and a feeble scratching were heard at the door. Rushing out, the shepherd saw that the collie had brought in her share of the flock with not a single sheep missing. Then he noticed that the collie carried something in her mouth. He called her and she came and laid at his feet a new-born puppy.

Off she went into the snow again, but soon returned with another puppy, but as she took this to her master she fell to the ground and died. James Hogg knew that although his faithful collie had had her puppies in a snowstorm she had carried out her duty to her master and had brought the sheep safely home.

1. What work did James Hogg do besides writing poetry?
2. What happened when he was out with his sheep one night?
3. How did the shepherd call his collie?
4. What did he tell her to do?
5. What did the shepherd do when he returned with the sheep?
6. What did he hear at the door of his cabin after waiting for several hours?
7. What did he see when he rushed out?
8. What happened to the collie when she brought back the second puppy?